31

Tips to Becoming an Effective Presenter

Tips to Becoming an Effective Presenter

Frank (Francesco) S. Adamo

TATE PUBLISHING & *Enterprises*

Published by Tate Publishing & Enterprises, LLC
127 E. Trade Center Terrace | Mustang, Oklahoma 73064 USA
1.888.361.9473 | www.tatepublishing.com

Tate Publishing is committed to excellence in the publishing industry. The company reflects the philosophy established by the founders, based on Psalm 68:11,

"The Lord gave the word and great was the company of those who published it."

Book design copyright © 2008 by Tate Publishing, LLC. All rights reserved.
Cover design by Kellie Southerland
Interior design by Stephanie Woloszyn

Published in the United States of America

ISBN: 978-1-60604-142-0
1. Language Arts & Discipline: Public
08.06.18

Acknowledgments

I want to acknowledge two people for their support and encouragement. First, I deeply appreciate my wife, Celly Feraren Adamo, who has put up with me, through thick and thin, for more than thirty-five years. Since 2002, I've been transitioning from being a business consultant to becoming a communications coach, trainer, speaker, and now, an author. During this transition, she stood by me as I continually worked on finding my passion. All of this while raising two grandkids who are now typical teenagers. She helped me edit and proof this book.

I also wish to acknowledge a person who is an accredited speaker and an internationally top rated trainer, speaker, and author: Sheryl Roush, the founder of Sparkle Presentations. I started this journey when another friend, professional speaker and my mentor, Jack Nichols introduced Sheryl and her workshops to me. I had been a Toastmaster, a member of a worldwide communication and leadership organization called Toastmasters International, for about ten years, but Sheryl's workshops took me to a new level that *sparked* a passion that had laid dormant for decades. Though it has been a long journey from that first spark, I believe I am well on the way to fulfilling my passion.

I also wish to thank all those who have helped me review and proof my book. I especially want to thank Dr. Dilip Abayasekara, an accredited speaker, professional speaker, trainer, speech coach, and the 2005–2006 Toastmasters International President. Perhaps we connected because both of us were chemists (I have a M.S. degree in analytical chemistry and he has a Ph.D. in organic and polymer chemistry.) Regardless, I am grateful for his support and review.

Next, I want to acknowledge fellow Toastmasters in Founder's District: Carl Walsh, who has such a way with words; Dr. Frannie Stein, who was such an inspiration with her enthusiastic support; Michelle Alba-Lim, a good friend and an accomplished speaker; Dr. Patricia Adelekan, an educator who checked my grammar and helped edit this book; and Mary G. Russell, immediate past District One Governor of Toastmasters. Last, but certainly not least, I want to thank Richard Ross, an accomplished proofreader, who seemed to find errors each time he proofed this book.

Additional books to follow:

31 Steps to Transcend your Presentation Fears

31 Tips to becoming a Presentainer

31 Tips in using PowerPoint Effectively

31 Tips to becoming an Effective Networker

31 Presentation Tips for Chemists, Engineers, and other Scientists

Table of Contents

Preface

When I was about ten, I was shy, a prime example of an introvert. One evening, the PTA had a magician entertain the kids. I was so amazed with the show and quite comfortable sitting on the floor and watching him perform. Then the magician asked for volunteers. Why I volunteered, I will never know. On the stage, all my excitement changed to fear. I was so terrified, my whole body froze and I couldn't speak. To my embarrassment, he had to call on another volunteer—my friend—to help him. I was not that terrified again but I maintained a fear of being in front of an audience for many years.

Have you been asked, or told, to give a presentation at work, at an event, or for a community organization? Perhaps you've been asked to participate in an interactive seminar and you simply felt uncomfortable.

Perhaps you are an experienced presenter but you've been presenting information rather than engaging the audience. As a chemist and as a computer consultant, I gave presentations during my career; however, I hardly interacted with the audience. I merely presented the information. Generally, I would stand behind the lectern while the slides projected onto a screen placed in the center of the room much like the photo below.

At the time, I really preferred this setup because I didn't feel comfortable giving a presentation, and the more the focus was off me and on the slides, the better I felt. Do you feel that way?

In my experience, many scientists, engineers, computer gurus, doctors, entrepreneurs, and many others are very knowledgeable in their vocation or business but they are uncomfortable in doing presentations. They do not have the experience of speaking to groups. Most likely, they, like me, did not take any workshops or classes in communication skills. If they had to speak to an audience, they simply learned by trial and error or from their peers who knew no more than they did.

This book is for those who are reluctant to deliver presentations and for those who want and need to understand the techniques of presenting effectively and want to improve their presentation skills.

Introduction

I consider "speakers" as professionals who are paid to motivate and inspire audiences. Speakers appear confident and are comfortable in speaking to large groups. They usually don't use notes or visual aids. They do not stand behind a lectern. Rather, they "work" and entertain the audience by interacting with them.

The vast majority, perhaps more than 90%, of those who speak in front of groups are, in my opinion, presenters, not professional speakers. They have the technical knowledge and, because of their work position, are required (whether they enjoy it or not) to present to others within their own work environment (i.e. to their staff, coworkers, or upper level management). They also may have to present to potential and current customers at trade shows, conventions, and other events, at public hearings such as city councils and planning commissions, and to the public at large.

Most presenters have no interest in becoming professional speakers; however, they do want to improve their presentation skills. An effective presentation is well written, adequately practiced, and skillfully delivered. If you are a presenter and you want to understand how to be more effective in your presentation, this book is for you. Enjoy.

Preparing your Presentation

1

Writing your Presentation

We write our presentation to refine it, to massage it, to rearrange it, to organize it better, and to remove verbiage that is not necessary.

Sometimes it's a struggle, but we really need to write our speeches. Some will write their presentation to memorize it or to read it. I saw a government agency representative deliver his presentation by reading the entire script. His presentation was supposed to be persuasive, but how can you be persuasive if you read the script? You really can't. I have seen other top executives and entrepreneurs memorize their speeches and get flustered when they lose their place.

We shouldn't write our speeches to read them or to memorize them. Certainly, there may be times we must read our speeches. The president of the United State needs to read the State of the Union Address because any slight variation may be misunderstood. Newscasters read the news using Teleprompters. We may also want to memorize the opening statement of a speech but not the entire speech.

We write our presentation for two basic reasons. One is the more obvious, to help us practice and rehearse our presentation. The other, and the more important reason, is to rewrite it. We write our presentation to rewrite it? Yes.

We write our presentation to refine it, to massage it, to rearrange it, to organize it better, and to remove verbiage that is not necessary. For example, I assisted another Toastmaster with his speech. He had written:

"Let me tell you about Mary Smith. Mary Smith lives…" I changed it to:

"Ask Mary Smith. She lives…" Not only did I reduce the verbiage from ten to five words, it became more active in tone.

2

Starting with the Conclusion

If your intent is to persuade, consider writing the conclusion first.

Most presenters will generally begin writing the opening, followed by the details, supporting data, and then finish by writing the conclusion. This is okay, especially if your intent is simply to inform. However, if your intent is to persuade, consider writing the conclusion first.

What is your call to action? What concepts do you want to leave the audience? WIIFM (What's In It For Me)–as a member of the audience? What is the specific purpose of your talk?

With these questions in mind, develop a call to action. For example, if you have a source to secure the future for retiring couples, such as reverse mortgages, you might end your presentation with, "Don't wait until you've retired to secure peace and tranquility for the rest of your life. Call us and invest in your future now!" Then add the facts and supporting data. Finish with an attention-getting opening such as, "Are you secured in your retirement years? If not, I have a three-step plan…"

3
Using the Power of Three

Of all odd numbers, three seems to be the "ideal" and, perhaps, the most powerful.

For some reason, unapparent to me, odd numbers have more impact than even numbers. We tend to remember odd things in our lives rather than mediocre (even) things. It's better to talk about three, five, or seven topics of interest rather than two, four, or six topics. The title of Stephen R. Covey's book is *The 7 Habits of Highly Effective People*. There is an eighth habit, but it is a separate book with one (odd number) additional habit.

Of all odd numbers, three seems to be the "ideal" and, perhaps, the most powerful number for the number of topics in a speech or presentation. We structure our presentations with an opening, a body, and a conclusion—a group of three sections. One way to structure a speech is to tell the audience what we're going to tell them, tell them again, and tell them what we told them—tell them three times.

If we are well organized, we can deliver an effective and meaningful talk. Grouping our topics and subtopics into groups of three, will help us to be better organized. For example, if you want to encourage your city council to build a skateboard park near the city hall, you might have the following outline:

Topic Outline: In Favor of Skateboard Park

1. A place for our Youth

    a. Keep our kids off the streets
        1) Reduced gang activities
        2) Fewer confrontations
        3) More interaction with peers and adults

    b. A place for positive activities
        1) Replacement for drug activities
        2) Better grades in school
        3) Positive interactions with others

    c. Future considerations

2. More Family Interaction

3. Personal Growth

A bonus of grouping our presentations into topics of three is that it is easier to know where we are in the presentation. If we are sidetracked, we can more easily return to where we were.

4

Grabbing the Audience's Attention

Grab the audience's attention immediately, then if there's a need, compliment or thank the organizers and the audience.

How long do we have to grab the audience's attention? David Ogilvy, author of *Confessions of an Advertising Man,* and others have said as little as seven seconds. Others say ten to fifteen seconds. Surely, we have no more than thirty seconds to capture our audience's attention.

Yet, how many times have we seen someone begin with a statement such as, "Thank you, Mr. Chairperson, for allowing me to speak this evening. Ladies and gentlemen, I'm honored to be here tonight to discuss this most pressing issue, preventing fires during the driest season we have had for years." This would take about ten seconds to say. Ten seconds to get to the point. Ten seconds before the audience begins to answer, "Why am I here?"

Instead, grab the audience's attention immediately, then, if there's a need, compliment or thank the organizers and the audience. For example, say something like, "Last year during the dry season, our region lost two precious lives, one hundred acres of forest land, and $20 million in property damage. This year, by enacting my common sense program, we can make sure that, during this dry season, history will not repeat itself. Thank you, Mr. Chairperson, welcomed guests, and fellow neighbors; I have a three-step program. First, we need to clear the dry brush around our homes…"

What are some attention getters? Here are some examples:

- *Explain why the topic is important*
  "We need to address global warming because…"

- *Make a surprising statement*
  "We need to disband our organization—now!"

- *Create suspense or curiosity*
  If the topic was fear of public speaking, we might begin with, "It seemed like slow motion as I walked up to the lectern. Each step I took was like walking in quicksand. By the time I reached the lectern, I thought my heart had stopped!"

- *Tell a story or anecdote*

    It was an eerie Sunday morning as I was waking up to my radio alarm. "Kennedy has been shot! Kennedy has been shot!" Was I dreaming? I seemed stuck in the Twilight Zone, as I was reliving President Kennedy's assassination in slow motion. As I awoke, I realized that Bobby Kennedy had been shot. Have you been in a situation where you seemed to be dreaming, but you knew it was real?

- *Ask a rhetorical question*

    "Are you alive? Really alive and living your dream?"

- *Begin with a quotation*

    "President Kennedy said 'Ask not what your country can do for you; ask what you can do for your country.' Today, I ask you what you can do for our organization."

- *Refer to the occasion or the theme*

    An internationally known professional speaker, Sheryl Roush of Sparkle Presentations, adapts her presentation to the theme. When the theme was the "Wizard of Oz," she guided us down the yellow brick road. At another event, the theme was "Pirates," and we followed her treasure map. It was the same presentation but a different path.

5

Organizing Your Presentation

One of the easiest ways to organize your presentation is to create PowerPoint slides from Microsoft Word.

Have you been to a presentation where you asked yourself, "What?" or "Where is he/she going with this?" Perhaps you might have said to yourself, "Now, I am lost!"

To be effective, you need to give an organized and a well thought-out presentation. One of the easiest ways to organize your presentation is to create PowerPoint slides from Microsoft Word.

You can outline and organize your presentation in Word by switching the view mode to Outline then adding the topics by using the headings (i.e. Heading 1, Heading 2, etc.). Use Heading 1 for the main topics, Heading 2 for each of the subtopics, and so on. You can then switch back to normal view to add the contents for your presentation. Making use of the example in Tip 3, that is:

Topic Outline: In Favor of Skateboard Park

1. A place for our Youth

    a. Keep our kids off the streets
        1) Reduced gang activities
        2) Fewer confrontations
        3) More interaction with peers and adults

    b. A place for positive activities
        1) Replacement for drug activities
        2) Better grades in school
        3) Positive interactions with others

    c. Future considerations

2. More Family Interaction

3. Personal Growth

You can generate a PowerPoint slideshow simply by clicking on: *File*, *Send To* and then *Microsoft Office PowerPoint*.

PowerPoint will open and display the PowerPoint slides based on each heading. Heading 1 will be the title; Heading 2 will be the main topic points; and Heading 3 the subtopic points, etc. as shown in the examples below:

A Place for our Youth
Keep our kids off the streets

- Reduced gang activities

- Fewer confrontations

- More interaction with peers and adults

A Place for our Youth
A place for positive activities

- Replacement for drug activities

- Better grades in school

- Positive interactions with others

Notice there is no background—the slides are black text on a white background. This is the perfect time to print the slides and use the printouts as your outline.

To print out a copy of the slides for your outline, go to *File*, *Print* and then choose *Slides* where it states "*Print what:*" Then print the slides. This will give you one slide per page. If you want to have two slides per page, then choose *Handouts* where it states "*Print what:*" and then choose 2 where it states "*Slides per page.*"

If you plan to use PowerPoint in your presentation then choose a background and design, etc. according to the PowerPoint directions.

In summary, develop your presentation using headings for the topics and subtopics, convert the headings to a PowerPoint file, and then use the slide printouts for your outline.

6

Practicing Without Visual Aids

PowerPoint and other visual aids should be used only to enhance your presentation—not to distract from it.

Certainly, a picture is worth a thousand words and visual aids are important and may be essential. However, once you have outlined and organized your presentation, you should practice your presentation without PowerPoint or any other visual aids. You should develop your body language and vocal variety to illustrate the scenes and engage the audience. Why, you may ask.

What if you have prepared for a PowerPoint presentation and everything seemed to go wrong? I have. I was giving a speech at my Toastmasters club. The title of the speech was *How to Give an Effective Business Presentation.*

Unfortunately, Murphy, of Murphy's Law Inc., came with me to the meeting. I was running late and, even though I arrived a few minutes before the meeting started, I was unable to connect my laptop to the large screen TV. When I was introduced, I quickly placed my laptop on top of the TV and began using the laptop screen to show my PowerPoint slides. About two minutes into the presentation, the laptop crashed—just as I was talking about having a backup system such as having a printed copy of the slides for notes. Guess what? Remember, I said I was running late. I didn't bring my backup!

I was able to continue because I had practiced; however, although everything seemed to have gone wrong, my very important informative speech became the most humorous speech I ever gave—and I'm not a funny guy.

More importantly, the center of attention should always be on you, the presenter, not on cutesy displays. Regretfully, many presenters concentrate on enhancing their PowerPoint slides rather than their own presentations. As a result, the slide show becomes the focus.

PowerPoint and other visual aids should be used *only to enhance* your presentation, not to distract from it. In fact, once you have rehearsed your presentation without visual aids, review your visual materials and remove any slides, etc., which *do not* enhance your presentation.

7

Rehearsing Your Presentation

To rehearse is similar to a dress rehearsal before the opening of a play.

Why do I say rehearse since I've already discussed practicing your presentation? Practice is just that. We can practice in the shower, in the car, at work, nearly anywhere. We just have to be cautious not to distract the people around us.

To rehearse is akin to a dress rehearsal before the opening of a play. If you are presenting outside your work environment, find the opportunity to rehearse at the location where you will be presenting. If you will be presenting at work, find the time to rehearse in the assigned room, even though you are familiar with it. You can also rehearse at home in your living or family room. Arrange the room with chairs, etc. where it simulates a room full of people. Also, dress accordingly. If it is a suit and tie event, dress in a suit and tie. If you will be speaking at a black-tie event, dress up in your formal wear even though you may want to be comfortable at home in trousers and a sweatshirt.

Preparing for your Presentation

Where will you present?

In a lecture hall, in a boardroom, or in a large auditorium?

8
Creating a Checklist

You should develop a checklist specific to your own needs.

Not only should we prepare our presentation, we also need to prepare for our presentation. If you are presenting at your own facility, you may have some knowledge of the room, the equipment, and the audience, but it still makes sense to check with those managing the room and equipment to ensure that everything is ready.

Certainly, if you are presenting at an outside venue, contact the team in charge of the room and equipment. Some items you should have on your checklist may include:

- Laptop (perhaps an extra laptop)
- Backup CD, flash drive and/or a hard copy printout of your visual aids (such as PowerPoint slides)
- Extra power cords, cables, bulbs, CDs and other accessories for your laptop and other equipment. (include a monitor-to-PC

extension cord to ensure that you have enough length to connect your laptop to a facility's multimedia equipment.)

- Contact person, including the person's cell phone number, for the computer/multimedia equipment to assure that technical assistance will be available if you will be using the facility's equipment.

- Introduction for the person introducing you; in fact, will someone be introducing you?

- Your audience (young, seasoned, male, female, or both genders, etc.)

- Layout of the room (round tables, theatre style chairs with no tables, tables perpendicular to the wall or skewed slightly for better viewing, etc.)

- Location of your projector and screen

- Your printed materials, including your evaluation forms

- Will you need a microphone and will the facility's management provide a microphone or should you?

- Will there be a lectern available and where will it be located?

These are just a few items for a checklist. You should develop a checklist specific to your own needs.

9

Knowing Your Location

Don't assume that everything is set up.

Have you ever gone to a familiar venue, such as a hotel, to give a presentation and you were surprised by the layout of the room? Even if you are familiar with the facility, you should check it out beforehand.

Perhaps you arrived at a location with barely any time to set up your equipment and realized that the tables and/or chairs were *not* conducive to your talk? For example, you were prepared to have your audience write notes or to fill out forms during your presentation, and there are no tables or clipboards to aid in writing.

I was scheduled to do a training session at a very familiar hotel. Based on a previous presentation, I assumed I was going to present in the same room and the room layout would be "U" shaped. I arrived early but not early enough. First, I was not scheduled to speak in the room

I expected. Then, it took me at least ten minutes to find the other room. The management failed to change the sign for the room that indicated the room was for another organization. When I arrived, the room was set up in an elongated boardroom fashion: a very long and narrow table—an extremely poor layout for presenting. I had no time to change the layout, thus I had to speak from the center of the table. It was an awkward setting. I hoped that those near me wouldn't lose their hearing while I raised my voice to assure I would be heard at the end of the table. I could have presented from one end of the table but the attendees at the far end would have had real difficulty hearing me. By the way, there was no microphone.

If you are unfamiliar with the venue, especially if it is not local, consider arriving the day before. I had a presentation to give in the Tampa Bay area in Florida. Tampa is my hometown and I am quite familiar with the Tampa Bay area, but I hadn't been back for about seven years. I arrived at night, and the first thing I did in the morning was *not* visit my relatives. Rather, I left to locate the venue where I would be presenting. Sure enough, I got lost. It took me nearly an hour to locate the facility that was only fifteen minutes away. What would I have done if I had waited until the day of the event to locate the venue?

When I arrived at the location site in St. Pete, I located the room where I was scheduled to speak. The room was set up with everything I needed, including a computer and a projector. I tried my CD and it worked well. Everything was great, except that the room was three times larger than I had expected. I had expected about thirty attendees but the room was set up for more than one hundred people. I had handouts for only thirty-five. Fortunately, I was able to find the event coordinator and he assured me that the big room would be set up as three small rooms.

Perhaps you will be presenting at your work environment. Even then, don't assume that everything is set up. About an hour before you plan to present, walk down the hallway (or wherever you are scheduled to speak) and check to verify that everything is ready for your presentation.

I've been teaching at Cypress College for more than three years, two years in the same room. I returned in the fall and, sure enough, the room layout was different. Fortunately, I arrived early enough to rearrange the chairs to conform to my needs.

10

Familiarizing Yourself with Your Audience

Even if you know all your attendees, take a few moments before the presentation to greet them.

In many cases, you will know your audience because you are presenting within your workplace or organization. However, when you are presenting outside your office, such as at a business conference, you most likely will not be familiar with your audience. Then what do you do?

Arrive early and check the room for any last-minute changes. Then, take a short break and get ready to meet your audience. Take notes of anything you might want to add to your presentation, particularly the names of those you meet. Then, if appropriate, adapt your presentation to include some of the individuals in your audience.

For example, you are presenting a paper on cancer research and you just met the leading authority in breast cancer research. You could announce, at the appropriate moment in your presentation, that you met Dr. so and so. "He's here in the audience. Please stand up." Then you can proceed to let the audience know of your brief conversation. Of course, the conversation needs to support your presentation but you've recognized a leader in cancer research, which can raise the audience's respect for you.

An added advantage of stating names of those in your audience is that you personalize your message. For example, you might say something like, "John and I were talking a few minutes ago and he had a great point…"

Even if you are presenting at your workplace, take a few moments before the presentation to greet those attending. In the course of mingling with your audience, something may come up that would be appropriate to discuss in your presentation. You can also familiarize yourself with any special guests who may be attending your presentation, such as potential customers you have not met in person.

Your Presentation

11

Positioning the Projector and Screen

To be an effective presenter, you want to be the center of attention, to be able to present from the center of the staging area.

Unfortunately, most screens are positioned directly in the center of the staging area, as illustrated in Figure 1. You may ask, "But what's wrong with this arrangement?" This seems like a typical layout of a room for a PowerPoint presentation. The screen is in the middle of the room with a wide center aisle. The projector is "properly" placed on the table directly in front of the screen and the lectern is to one side or the other. Though this is the typical layout for many presentations, the presenter generally stands behind the lectern while the screen becomes the focal point. As I have already mentioned, you, the presenter, should be the focus of your own presentation. You are the authority. You are the expert. You are giving the message. How can you be the *center of attention,* especially if the room is dimmed to highlight the screen and you are barely visible?

Figure 1: Typical room layout for a presentation

Furthermore, how many times have you seen a presenter walk in front of the projector and block the view of the screen? Worse yet, the audience may be distracted, not only by the screen being blocked, but also by having the projector's bright light shining on your chest or below.

On the other hand, to be an effective presenter, you want to be the center of attention, to be able to present from the center of the staging area. In the above scenario, you would be quite limited to the audience's left side. Even if you wanted to move out and away from the lectern and expand the staging area, you couldn't without blocking the screen.

Figure 2: This is the ideal layout for an effective presentation

Consider placing your screen in the corner of the room as shown in Figure 2. Actually, this is the ideal layout for a presentation. Not only is the screen in the corner, there is a raised podium (the platform). The lectern is located toward the rear and to one side of the podium allowing room for you, the presenter, to move about without interrupting any part of your slide show. Thus, you will be the center of attention, not the screen as in Figure 1.

For your information, both figures are photos of the same room, only the layout is different. The layout above was set up for the 2007 Toastmasters

International Convention in Phoenix, AZ. The former layout, Figure 1, was set up for another organization.

12
Using the Lectern

Many presenters will stand behind the lectern when they present. If you have the opportunity, move away from the lectern and closer to the audience.

Presenting from the lectern is very common but not particularly effective. Regardless of what we are presenting, we are, at least for the moment, the experts on the topic we are giving. Unfortunately, when we present from the lectern, particularly if you have visual aids such as PowerPoint, the attention of the audience is generally on the screen, not us; therefore, we are not as effective as we can be.

Many presenters will stand behind the lectern when they present. If you have the opportunity, move away from the lectern and closer to the audience. As you do this, you will engage the audience. You will go from being a presenter to becoming a conversationalist. That's a major key to becoming an effective presenter. Additionally, you will be able to engage the entire audience rather than just the portion of the audience from where you are presenting.

Occasionally, you may be presenting at the head table and you have little room to move away from the lectern. If possible, ask if you can present from the floor or perhaps there is already a podium off to the side where you can give your presentation.

13

Pausing Before Beginning

*Take a moment or two and pause
before you begin your presentation.*

You need to grab your audience's attention before
beginning your presentation; otherwise, our
speech opener may go unnoticed. Many times
individuals in the audience may begin to converse
with one another. That is just natural. By pausing
a moment or two before you begin, the audience
will quiet down. This will relax you and it will get
the audience's attention.

Once you have reached the lectern or the
staging area, don't simply stare at the audience.
Make eye contact with the entire audience.
There's just enough time to "scan" the room
from left to right and then return to the center.
"Scan" is in quotation marks to emphasize not
to scan the room with robotic eyes. Merely
smile and make eye contact with individuals in
a personalized manner. By the time you have
reached the right side of the room, you should

"hear" the silence of anticipation. Now, you have the audience's attention. Now, the audience will not miss your opening. Now, you can begin.

14

Apologizing

Remember, you are the expert. People came to hear you speak. If you acknowledge a mistake, it may lower the expectation of your audience.

Have you ever forgotten part of your presentation, and you stopped and said something like, "Oops! I forgot to explain…" Perhaps, you started your presentation with something like, "Sorry, I'm not totally prepared. We had this rush job yesterday, and I simply didn't have the time to prepare for this morning's presentation…" Perhaps you just joined a Toastmasters club, and you realized you said an "ah," "um," or "you know" and you announce it to the audience. "Oops, I just said an ah!" If you are a bit nervous and, in your mind, you are sweating, your knees are shaking, and your lips are quivering, just carry on with your presentation because most members of the audience will not notice.

If you forget something, perhaps you can include it later in the presentation. If not, then simply skip it. Most likely, no one will notice, so why acknowledge a mistake during your presentation. Remember, you are the expert. People came to hear you speak. If you acknowledge a mistake, it may lower the expectation of your audience.

On the other hand, if you stumble as you walk up to the lectern or you get startled by a waiter dropping the dishes or if an alarm goes off then, by all means, acknowledge the incident. Add a bit of humor. For example, if an alarm goes off, say something like, "Is God telling me my time's up?" as you look at your watch and then look up.

Lilly Walters, executive director of Walters International Speakers Bureau, wrote a book titled *What to Say When...You're Dying on the Platform*. This book covers nearly everything that could happen during your presentation with both serious and humorous suggestions of how to handle those situations.

15
Using PowerPoint or Other Visual Aids

> *PowerPoint is a tremendous tool that*
> *should not be ignored, but the slides*
> *need to enhance our presentation and*
> *not detract from the ultimate goal of*
> *our message.*

As I have mentioned before, the attention of your audience, during your presentation, should always be on you, the presenter, not on some cutesy displays. PowerPoint and other visual aids should be used *only* to *enhance* your presentation, not to distract from it.

Have you been mesmerized by a simply amazing PowerPoint presentation, but, after you left the presentation, you asked yourself, "What did he talk about?" Perhaps you attended a presentation where the presenter simply read detailed text that was shown on the slides. Perhaps you attended one where each slide began with a chime or some other sound. It was cute for the first few slides but, after the umpteenth time, it was simply too distracting.

PowerPoint is a tremendous tool that should not be ignored, but the slides need to enhance our presentation and not detract from the ultimate goal of our message.

What happens if the projector bulb burns out or you can't connect your laptop to the projector? Are you prepared to continue your presentation without PowerPoint?

I've had problems with my laptop recently. With my grandkids using the laptop, it had slowed to a crawl. Even the thickest molasses dripped faster than my laptop would boot up. I would still take the laptop to my class or workshop, but it took so long to boot up, I finally turned it off and proceeded without it. Interestingly, my students told me I did a better job without my PowerPoint slides. Why? Very simply, I was more engaged. I was totally focused on their needs, and I adjusted the training to accommodate them.

PowerPoint is an extremely powerful tool. Use it to enhance your presentation, not to detract from it. Most importantly, don't rely on it. When Murphy shows up, Murphy's Law will take over. I know. I've been there, and I had to be prepared to proceed without the PowerPoint slides.

16
Using Outlines

If you leave the lectern to engage the audience, you can always return to the lectern, quickly glance at the outline, and continue with the next topic without interruption.

Have you seen people read their presentation or, having memorized their talk, they lost their place because a waiter dropped the dishes or an alarm sounded? Additionally, if you memorize your speech, it may sound canned: like a telemarketer reciting a script; thus, you may not connect with the audience. If you read your presentation, you will *not* connect with the audience. Then, what do you do?

First, practice, practice, and then practice some more. The more we practice the better the presentation. In Tip 3, I discussed the power of three. By arranging your presentations in groups of three, you can easily keep track of where you are in your presentation.

In another earlier tip, Tip 5, I suggested that you write your presentations in Word, create a set of PowerPoint slides, and then print the PowerPoint slides and use the printed copy as your notes.

Why are printed copies of your PowerPoint slides so effective as notes? First, the notes are simple to create from your written presentation. Second, the notes are very easy to see with the size of the fonts ranging from an average of twenty-four to forty-four points. Third, you will only have three or four topic headings per sheet—making it easy to keep on track. Thus, when you leave the lectern to engage the audience, you can always return to the lectern, quickly glance at the outline and continue with the next topic without interruption.

17

Avoiding Jargon or Acronyms

Refrain from using your industry's jargon, abbreviations, or acronyms, even if you are presenting in front of colleagues.

EDTA, EthyleneDiamineTetraacetic Acid, is a commonly known chelating agent and water softener in the chemical, medical, and water softener industries. Water companies may use EDTA but the personnel may not know the chemistry involved. If I were to present research to reveal a more powerful chelating agent, i.e. DTPA, should I have to define EDTA? Would I have to describe DTPA, (DiethyleneTriaminePentaacetic Acid) because it is a lesser-known chelating agent? What should I do if I was presenting to a water softener company with the ultimate goal of selling them DTPA? If I was to present to the public, how should I present it? Perhaps I have to persuade the city council to use DTPA rather than EDTA. The council members may not even know anything about "chelating," let alone, the abbreviations.

Even to a chemist, I could explain in simpler terms, "EDTA is a chemical that will wrap around metal ions such as calcium and magnesium, much like a spider wraps its prey with its web. In turn, these metals can be replaced by sodium ions, which will soften the water. DTPA is simply a chemical like EDTA which is stronger and more efficient—and the cost is only slightly more than EDTA."

I can even simplify the message to the public by just mentioning that this chemical is more efficient than the current chemical the city is using. There really is no reason to mention EDTA or DTPA if I explain the effects in simple terms.

To be effective in your presentation, refrain from using your industry's jargon, abbreviations, or acronyms, even if you are presenting in front of colleagues. However, if you do, explain the term(s) in simple and understandable language.

18
Doing your Research

Do your research. Learn about the client. Understand who they are and what they do.

If you are presenting to a potential client, or even to a current client, be diligent and do your research. Learn about the client. Understand who they are and what they do. Get to know their industry.

If you are presenting to a specific company or industry, consider using inherent terminology to let them know that you have been diligent in researching their industry. For example, if you are marketing a software product to realtors, you may say, "Our product is so efficient, it will expedite your *farming* process tenfold." Be extremely careful, however, that you really understand the phrases you include in your presentations and how they fit in your audience's industry. The word "farming" has a different meaning to the fish industry and a totally different meaning to baseball.

19
Making Eye Contact

Eye contact is extremely important to the audience.

Have you been to a presentation where the speaker reads his/her speech without looking up? Perhaps the presenter stood behind the lectern and gazed out into the audience but never made direct eye contact with you or the others. I watched a professor from a well-known university give his presentation. He had appropriate body language and great vocal variety, but he had little, if any, eye contact with the audience. He was wonderful to listen to, but I was distracted. I was focused on his eyes, waiting to see if he would make direct eye contact with any member of the audience.

On the other hand, I saw a speaker give his talk at a Toastmasters club, and throughout his speech, he seemed to have terrific eye contact. He really engaged the audience with his speech. After finishing his speech, he returned to his seat, which was directly across from me. He listened intently to the other speakers and his evaluator. His eyes were focused on the other speakers and evaluators during the entire meeting. It was only after the meeting that he folded out his cane—a white cane with a red tip used by the blind. I absolutely had no idea that the speaker was blind.

When we converse with one another, we make eye contact to show that we are engaged in the conversation. If we look away, it may indicate that we are distracted, and our attention is elsewhere. Likewise, when giving a presentation, we should make eye contact with the audience. Eye contact is essential because it helps us, as presenters, to connect with the audience. However, if you are a bit fearful speaking to groups, you may tend to refrain from eye contact. You may feel the audience is *staring* back at you and it will heighten your fear. On the contrary, engaging the audience through effective eye contact will lessen your fear because the audience will be more attentive.

To be effective, focus on one person (or a small group in a large audience) for three to four seconds, and then make eye contact with another person (or small group) for another three to four seconds as if conversing with each individual. If you are a bit uncomfortable, then find someone in the audience you know or one who shows interest by smiling or nodding.

At the very minimum, focus your eyes at or just above the eyebrows. You will feel more comfortable, and direct eye contact will become natural as you give more presentations.

20
Understanding Different Cultures

In general, we can make direct eye contact with Middle Easterners, some Latin Americans, and the French. Refrain from making direct eye contact with East Asians, Southeast Asians, East Indians, and Native Americans.

In some Asian countries, direct eye contact is considered rude and aggressive. In other countries, such as some Arab countries, eye contact among men is even more important than in the U.S. Eye contact is highly respected between men, but making eye contact with or staring at women is highly disrespectful. In America, and most European countries, eye contact is natural and expected, but we should refrain from staring or gazing.

In general, we can make direct eye contact with Middle Easterners, some Latin Americans, and the French. Americans, Northern Europeans, and the British are comfortable with eye contact but in some moderation. Refrain from making direct eye contact with East Asians, Southeast Asians, East Indians, and Native Americans.

If you are presenting in another country or to a specific group of people from another country where eye contact may be considered rude, be considerate of their culture and use eye contact in moderation. On the other hand, don't overly exaggerate your eye contact with those who expect and respect direct eye contact.

Additionally, be cautious of other cultural customs other than eye contact, such as body language and voice variety. For example, being soft spoken may be disquieting in some cultures, yet well received in others. Engaging the audience by asking questions or role-playing may be acceptable in American and other cultures, but may be considered rude in some.

Always be diligent and research cultural differences if you are presenting in another country or you are presenting to a group from another country. If, for some reason, you do offend someone, don't try to make excuses or go into a long, drawn out explanation. Simply, be honest and apologize. Explain diplomatically that you were not aware that the incident was offensive and knowing now what it meant, it won't happen again.

21

Focusing on Benefits, Not Features

Benefits emotionalize features.

Features describe the product or service. They are independent of the audience. Benefits describe what the products or services will do for the audience. One method of getting from features to benefits is to ask "So what?" or "Who cares?"

My workshops focus on identifying the key issues for delivering effective business presentations. Features of my workshops may include:

- Instructor has been a member of Toastmasters since 1991

- The workshops are engaging and interactive

- The workshops are held in the evenings to accommodate people who work during the day

A prospective audience member may ask me, "So what?" Just because I've been a Toastmaster since 1991, how will that help him? "It's great that the workshops are engaging and interactive, but what will I learn from them?"

In contrast, the benefits of attending the workshops will answer those questions and may include:

- Reduce, minimize, and even eliminate your presentation fears
- Regain or bolster your confidence
- Close more sales with less effort

Let's take another example: an automobile that features eight airbags. Whoopee do! So what? However, what if you would explain, "With 8 airbags, this automobile will protect your family more than any other vehicle on the road." Eight airbags, then, is a feature that will benefit the buyer and his family.

In essence, benefits emotionalize features. For each feature, find the emotion that will benefit the audience. When you are giving a persuasive presentation, listen! For example, in a sales presentation, you may be discussing a list of benefits, but those may not be important to a potential customer. By listening to the group, you will be able to identify their specific needs and adjust your presentation to include the benefits they are seeking.

In a small sales presentation that's relatively easy to do by their verbal responses. However, how do you "listen" to a larger audience? "Listen" to their body language. For example, are their minds wandering (little eye contact) or are they attentive? Adjust your presentation accordingly.

22

Shortening Your Presentation

Have you been in a situation where there are a series of presenters and the scheduled events were running behind time?

One time I mistakenly scheduled two speakers for our Rotary club. Unfortunately, both speakers showed up. The first speaker trimmed his twenty-minute presentation to fifteen minutes. The latter speaker, even though he knew he would go overtime, gave his full talk. As a result, nearly a quarter of our members left before he finished. Other members stayed but many were fidgeting and did not stay focused on the speaker's presentation.

Have you been in a situation where there was a series of presenters and the scheduled events were running behind time? You would be the hero if you could cut ten minutes from your forty-five-minute presentation and help the event planners get back on track. But how?

Many professional presenters will have multiple versions of the same presentation ranging from perhaps a ten-minute speech to a two-day workshop. If you divide your presentation into groups of three topics, three subtopics, etc., (see Tip 3) it will be easier to eliminate one or two of the subtopics in midstream, particularly if you arrange the first subtopic as the most important and the third as the least important.

Another way to shorten your presentations is to have a series of mini speeches. Many speeches given by Toastmasters are five to seven minutes in length. Thus, if a Toastmaster is requested to deliver a forty-five-minute presentation, he/she could group together a series of six five- to seven-minute speeches. You can do the same.

One caution! Because each mini speech is a complete speech in itself with an opening, a body, and a conclusion, you will need to build a transition between the conclusion of one mini speech and the opening of the next mini speech. In addition, the initial opening and the final conclusion would also need to be modified to incorporate the overall theme and the purpose of the entire series of mini speeches. Then, if you only have thirty-five minutes rather than forty-five minutes for your presentation, you can readily remove one of the mini speeches and conclude on time.

23

Answering Questions

After a few questions and answers, your excitement from the powerful conclusion waned and you left without taking any action.

Have you been to a presentation where the speaker ended with a powerful conclusion, you were excited and ready to take action, and then the presenter asked something like, "Do you have any questions?" After a few questions and answers, your excitement from the powerful conclusion waned and you left without taking any action.

I've known many presenters, including myself, who concluded their presentations and then asked for questions. Though this seems to be a typical scenario, asking questions at the end will generally reduce the impact of a strong conclusion. Then, when do we answer questions?

Some presenters may be open to questions anytime during their presentation; however, they really need to be on top of their presentation to assure that they don't lose track and complete their presentation on time. This can be a challenge for many—even for the most experienced presenters.

Generally, the method I use is to ask for questions after each main topic. Typically, I will have an opening, a body, and a transitional conclusion for each main topic. At the end of each transitional topic, I will call for questions. For example, I may say, "Before continuing, do you have any questions?" Then I will take no more than three to four questions and proceed to the next topic. If appropriate, I may transition to the next topic by incorporating the last answer. At the end of my last topic, but before my final conclusion, I will ask for questions again.

If you use this method, check your watch to be sure you have enough time to finish your last conclusion without rushing. For example, if your conclusion will take five minutes, take your final questions eight to ten minutes from the end of your allotted time. This will allow three to five minutes to answer questions before starting your powerful conclusion. To let the audience know that you need to conclude the question and answer section, you can say something like, "I will take one more question," or "I'll be available after this presentation to answer any individual questions." Then, after answering the last question, proceed with your conclusion.

24
Distributing Handouts

My choice is to distribute the handouts at the end of the presentation.

Some presenters distribute their handouts as they begin their presentation. Consider not doing this! The beginning of your presentation is your attention getter. When handouts are distributed, the attention is on the handouts—not you. Invariably, some, if not most, of the members of the audience will flip through the handouts and read the information in the handouts rather than focusing on you. Occasionally, if they read ahead, some may spot their interest and mentally shut you out until you reach that specific topic.

Presenters may pass out worksheets in the middle of their presentations when they want to set up an exercise for the audience. This is acceptable; however, understand that this, again, can create a distraction.

Then when do you distribute handouts? In my opinion, you have two good choices. Distribute the handouts at the beginning *before* the presentation or have them available at the end of the presentation. My personal choice is to distribute the handouts at the end of the presentation. If the audience has nothing to view or flip through during a presentation, the focus will always be on you.

If you decide to have the handouts available at the end and you have some time after the presentation, have them available near you. If you must immediately exit the room for the next presenter, have the handouts near the back of the room or immediately outside the room. Either way, the audience will come to you to pick up the handouts, which will give you the opportunity to network with your audience. If you pass out your handouts before you begin, the audience has all the information they need. Thus, they may immediately exit and you'll miss the opportunity to mingle with them.

There's one additional bonus of waiting until the end of your presentation to distribute your handouts. If you need to shorten your presentation because of time constraints, they will be none the wiser and they will not feel short changed.

If you choose to distribute handouts before you start your presentation, distribute them face down. Then you can ask the audience to turn them over when you are ready to discuss the specifics included in your handouts.

25

Broadcasting Your Outline

Don't give any indication of your outline unless you have control of your time.

I give workshops and teach classes on effective communications. Generally, I have control of the time. I know how long I have to talk and I can plan for the total time period. Contrarily, you are *not* in control of your time—others are—when you are presenting at any outside event such as at a conference, at your client's office, etc.

One time I was scheduled to give a presentation at a chamber event. I had about forty minutes to speak. I prepared a handout with a series of statements with blank spaces for the audience to complete during my forty-minute presentation. On the day of the presentation, I arrived early and placed the handouts on all the tables; however, as the members and guests began to arrive, I was given only twenty minutes for my presentation—*half of my expected time*. Because I had passed out my "agenda," I felt I was caught between a rock and a hard place.

I thought, *Do I adjust my time to twenty minutes and ignore the list of statements I had passed out? Should I attempt to leave out the stories and just make the points? Could I simply rush through my presentation and conclude within twenty minutes? Or do I simply ignore the time constraint and take the full forty minutes like others had done – in the past?*

I managed to get through the presentation, and I ended on time, within the twenty minutes. The title of the workshop was *Effective Business Communications,* but was I effective? Others thought I did well, but in my opinion, I failed, not myself, but I failed the audience. One of the key methods to being effective is to converse with rather than present to the audience. Because I was figuring out how to close within twenty minutes, I was focusing on myself rather that the audience and my message. I ended up presenting to the audience rather than conversing with them.

As I mentioned, I didn't fail myself because I learned from this situation. One thing I learned is that you don't pass out any form of an "agenda:" a PowerPoint handout, a series of fill-in-the-blank statements, or an actual outline of your presentation *unless* you have control of your time or you are absolutely sure of your time allotment.

26

Learning From Every Presentation

If you were not effective in giving a presentation, be open-minded and learn from it.

In the last tip, Tip 25, I discussed how, in my opinion, I failed the audience at the chamber workshop. Note that I said I failed the audience. I don't consider that I failed. I would have failed if I had stopped giving presentations. Sure, I felt bad for a few days. However, I didn't fail because I got back on my feet, accepted what happened, and learned from my experience. We only fail if we stop doing what we are doing. Some say that Thomas Edison failed 5,000 times before he invented the light bulb. In my opinion, Edison never failed. He learned from each experiment and he continued with his work. Edison would have failed only if he stopped trying before the 5,000[th] time, but he persevered until he was successful in inventing the light bulb.

What did I learn from that experience? First, don't broadcast your "agenda" if you are not in control of the time. Secondly, and most important, no matter what happens, we need to focus on our message and our audience regardless of the situation. In my case, I could have explained that my handout was for a longer presentation and I would be available after the workshop to answer any topics not discussed. Then I could have continued with my presentation, attempting to cover as much material as I could, but always focusing on the audience.

What else did I learn? I learned to go with the flow. If I go with the flow, I can refocus my attention on the audience.

Ask for feedback but also evaluate your own performance. What was good? How can you improve? Audio/video tape your presentations. Analyze each tape as professional ball players analyze their past games. Ask yourself these and other questions. How was my voice? How were my gestures? Were my gestures appropriate? How can I improve on my gestures and voice? How many ahs and ums did I have? Did I fiddle with my tie or my hair this time? What could I have done differently?

Finally, always be open to suggestions. You have the option to accept them or not, but consider all of them.

27
Getting Feedback

Read the comments—even the negative comments.

What is the simplest way to learn from your presentations? Pass out evaluation forms. Do this when you are presenting at an event or other *non-sales type* meeting. You don't want to do this if your intent is to persuade a potential client to purchase a product or service. Something like, "Thank you for the purchase. Could you complete this form to let us know why you purchased the product?" would be inappropriate at the time of the sale.

There are many variations of an evaluation form but they all should contain at least three questions:

1. What did you like about the presentation?

2. What improvements could I make to improve the presentation?

3. Other comments

Additionally, you may include a table where the attendee can evaluate you from excellent to poor, or based on a score of 10 to 1 or 5 to 1. Some statements may include:

- Understood the subject matter
- Was well prepared
- Stimulated discussion and involvement within the group
- Was interesting and informative
- Provided individual help when needed

Read the comments—even the negative comments. Why would they say this? How can I improve my presentation based on these comments? Even though I thought I interacted with my audience, one comment kept popping up: more interaction, more exercises. Now I've extended one of my workshops from three to four hours to incorporate additional exercises.

If you happen to know of an experienced Toastmaster who will be attending your presentation, ask him/her to give you an evaluation after the presentation. Be open to the feedback and learn how well you did and how to improve on your future presentations.

Again, you don't want to ask for an evaluation immediately after you have closed a contract or product sale. However, a few days after you have closed the deal, you might call or write your customers, ask how they are doing with the product or service, and then ask if they have a moment to answer a few questions related to their purchase. It's also good PR to follow up with your clients.

Following the Presentation

28

Mingling With the Audience

We should mingle with the audience after our presentation. Of course, there may be times when this isn't possible, but if you can, you should.

In Tip 10, we learned to become familiar with our audience before our presentation. We should also mingle with the audience after our presentation. Of course, there may be times when this isn't possible, but if you can, you should. Even if the presentation is for your staff at work, take time to get feedback and to answer follow-up questions.

Answer questions? Didn't I mention not to answer questions at the end of your presentation? Yes, and that's exactly why you should stay around *after* your presentation. If you finish your presentation with a powerful conclusion, leaving your audience wanting more, they will want to see you after your presentation.

This is the time to follow up, distribute your handouts, answer additional questions, and sell products (back of the room sales) if you have products or services available. More than anything else, this is a great time to network and develop relationships with your audience. Depending on the circumstances, this may also be a perfect time to make an appointment or agree on a time to call to set an appointment.

Regretfully and too often, presenters, particularly when presenting to service clubs such as Rotary, Lions, and Kiwanis, leave immediately after their presentation and they lose their opportunity to network. In addition, the members of the service clubs are left with the taste (no pun intended) that your only interest was to get a free meal. That may not be true but be sure to take advantage of this opportunity to network and don't pass it up. Where else can you network when all the attention is on you?

29
Following Up

Be sure that you follow up within twenty-four to forty-eight hours.

Whenever you give an outside presentation, you should ask for business cards or have a contact information sheet for the audience to complete. If you have done this, be sure that you follow up within twenty-four to forty-eight hours.

To expedite updating your database with the newly collected business cards, purchase a card scanner, if you haven't done so already. I used to collect business cards, take them back to the office and…yes, I would stick them in the drawer. I still have bundles of business cards without email addresses, because email addresses never existed back then.

I'm certain that I have lost hundreds of thousands of dollars over the years simply because I failed to follow up. With a card scanner, all you have to do is pass the business cards through the card scanner, verify the information, and then, if you want, merge the data into your contact manager. It will take you less time to scan fifty business cards than to manually enter the data for five business cards. In my opinion, a card scanner is worth more than a pot of gold.

What should you do to follow up? In today's hi-tech environment, we can design an eloquent and personalized email to send to everyone and that is fine. However, the very best way is to follow up is with a handwritten note thanking that person for attending. It takes time to handwrite a short message, but the effort you take to do this will be highly appreciated. You might add a small statement asking them to contact you if they have a question or some concerns.

After the initial followup, schedule a series of reminders, perhaps a week, a month, three months later, etc. Whenever you have a new product or service, send a notice, and if this is done by email, always include an opt-out option.

Even if you do a presentation for your staff or upper management, you should also follow up. If you have spoken to your staff, follow up by asking if they fully understand the situation and if they have any questions, concerns, or even recommendations.

Other Tips

30
Evaluating Others

As you observe and evaluate others, learn from them—both the good and bad.

The first assignment I give in my classes is to evaluate someone at work, at home, or in the community. Observe someone attending a business meeting at work. Attend a free seminar. Watch a TV talk show or the PBS stations when they have speakers such as Wayne Dyer or Robert Kiyosaki. Even if you are not a Christian, you can certainly evaluate and learn communication skills from the ministers and preachers on Sunday morning or while watching the TBN Christian station. Watch a presentation on youtube.com. Just observe and evaluate someone, and ask yourself:

- Did the presenter have any ahs, ums, you knows, repeat words, etc.? How many?

- Did the presenter have voice modulations?

What were they, i.e. changes in pitch, pace, loudness, etc.? Were there deliberate pauses? Did he/she stretch a word or phrase (e.g. "I have seeeeeennn...") to enhance the message?

- Did the presenter use effective and appropriate gestures? Did he/she have too many gestures or not enough gestures?

- Did the presenter have an attention-getting opening? If so, what was it? Did you remember it a day or two later? Why or why not?

- Did the presenter have one clear message? What was it?

- Did the content support the presenter's message? How?

- What was the purpose of the presentation? Did you remember a day or two later? Why or why not?

- Was there a call to action or some other meaningful conclusion? What was it?

- Did you remember what the presenter wanted you to do a day or two later? Why or why not?

- Did the presenter tell stories? What were

they and did the stories help you remember the point of his/her presentation?

- How would you do it differently?

As you observe and evaluate others, learn from them—both the good and bad. For example, you may say to yourself, *I really like his eye contact and his voice modulations were great. His gestures, however, were abrupt and didn't coincide with his message. I'm going to work on my gestures. I have appropriate gestures, but they are somewhat abrupt.*

You may have observed that a presenter said a "you know" or an "ah" almost every ten seconds. You might think to yourself, *Wow, so many filler words. I didn't realize how distracting they were. I'm going to have to work on minimizing my ahs and ums.*

You may also have seen someone who was a dynamic speaker but, at the end, you'll ask yourself, *What was his message? He/she talked about this and that, but what was the point of the presentation?*

When you evaluate someone, don't be concerned about the actual content, particularly if the content is controversial and you have an opposite viewpoint. Just concentrate on how well he/she presented. Was he/she concise and organized? Did the presenter leave you intrigued, even though you had a different viewpoint? On the other hand, was the presenter merely giving a mishmash of rhetorical statements with no call to action? Was the presenter passionate and excited about his/her message, or was he/she merely loud and boring?

31

Joining Toastmasters

Toastmasters has helped millions of individuals gain confidence and poise by improving their communications and leadership skills.

Most, if not all, presenters are technically skilled and knowledgeable in their areas of expertise. In my opinion, however, many, especially those in engineering, science, and other hi-tech disciplines, have not had formal training in presentation skills. I know. I was in chemistry for thirteen years and in computer science for more than twenty years. I simply learned my "lack of" communication techniques from my co-workers and my superiors. Even if you took a speech, drama, or public speaking class (if one exists) in school, you probably never learned how to do presentations. Certainly, you may have given PowerPoint presentations and taken PowerPoint classes; however, being an expert in creating

PowerPoint presentations does nothing to prepare you for delivering an effective presentation.

Perhaps you do presentations, but you really don't feel comfortable talking in front of groups. Do you stand behind the lectern even though you have the room to move around the "staging" area? Do you rely on your PowerPoint slides to get you through your presentations? Have you noticed that you have a tendency to say "ahs," "ums" or "you knows" during your presentations? Do you avoid eye contact with your audience? Do you refrain from engaging the audience? If the answer is yes to any of these questions, then the answer is: *Join Toastmasters*

Go to *www.toastmasters.org*, click on "Find a location near you," which is located on the left-hand side and directly below Meeting Locations. Then enter your zip code if you are in the United States or Canada or select any of the more than ninety other countries. Toastmasters is the largest communications and leadership organization worldwide. Toastmasters has helped millions of individuals gain confidence and poise by improving their communications and leadership skills.

A Toastmasters meeting has three sections:

1. *Table Topics:* Table topics are mini impromptu speeches in which you are asked a question

and you have one to two minutes to answer. The question can be on any topic. What a great way to practice your skills for your questions and answers section of your presentation.

2. *Speeches:* Usually two to four members deliver prepared speeches from a manual. The length is generally five to seven minutes in length, but could be longer. Each manual speech has a specific purpose such as "Organize Your Speech," "Get to the Point," and "Research Your Topic." Isn't this a great place to practice your presentation in front of a supportive group?

3. *Evaluation:* The growth part of a Toastmasters meeting is the evaluation where another member evaluates your prepared speech. You will receive feedback on your strengths as a speaker and a couple of specific recommendations on how you might improve your speech. This is in contrast to your work environment where your co-workers may say, "You did a great job," even though you had little eye contact and you had seven "ahs" and two "you knows" in your speech, or you are criticized without any substantive feedback.

Overall, being a member of Toastmasters will improve your presentation skills, leadership skills, and your confidence through practice and through constructive and supportive feedback.